HARRY'S STORY

This beautifully illustrated picture book has been created to develop awareness of Developmental Language Disorder and provides a unique opportunity to sensitively gain children's perspectives of the condition.

Harry enjoys school, but faces daily challenges due to his language difficulties. When he is asked to write a story, he struggles to find the words to put his thoughts onto paper. He learns to share his stories through pictures instead and, in doing so, helps his supportive teacher understand what she can do to make life easier for him.

With bright illustrations and language that can be accessed by children with DLD, this story can be used to start conversations about the lived experience of children with Developmental Language Disorder, giving them a voice and helping them express their thoughts and feelings. It can also be used as a training tool for teachers and other professionals.

This is an essential resource for parents and practitioners looking to understand and support children with DLD.

Kate Kempton is a community speech and language therapist in Devon, who works with children in early years and school settings. Kate has a particular interest in Developmental Language Disorder and after completing a Masters in Language and Literacy at the University of Sheffield, became increasingly aware of the links between spoken and written language. This led to a further interest in narrative language and the importance of being able to tell and share our stories.

T0056246

Harry's Story

A Picture Book to Raise Awareness of and Support Children with DLD

Kate Kempton

To Sally, for teaching me the value of every child's experience,
and to see the world from their view.

Routledge
Taylor & Francis Group

LONDON AND NEW YORK

Cover image by Kate Kempton

First published 2022
by Routledge
4 Park Square, Milton Park, Abingdon, Oxon OX14 4RN

and by Routledge
605 Third Avenue, New York, NY 10158

Routledge is an imprint of the Taylor & Francis Group, an informa business

© 2022 Kate Kempton

British Library Cataloguing-in-Publication Data
A catalogue record for this book is available from the British Library

Library of Congress Cataloging-in-Publication Data
A catalog record for this book has been requested

ISBN: 978-1-032-17144-9 (pbk)
ISBN: 978-1-003-25197-2 (ebk)

DOI: 10.4324/9781003251972

Typeset in Antitled
by Apex CoVantage, LLC

Harry's Story

Story and pictures by
Kate Kempton

Harry is a little boy with a wide and happy smile.

But sounds and words are difficult,
so talking takes a while.

At school he likes his teacher
and his friends are really kind.

But words are hard to understand and
words are hard to find.

Miss Heart tells all the children what they will do today.
But it's noisy in the classroom and the words just fade away.

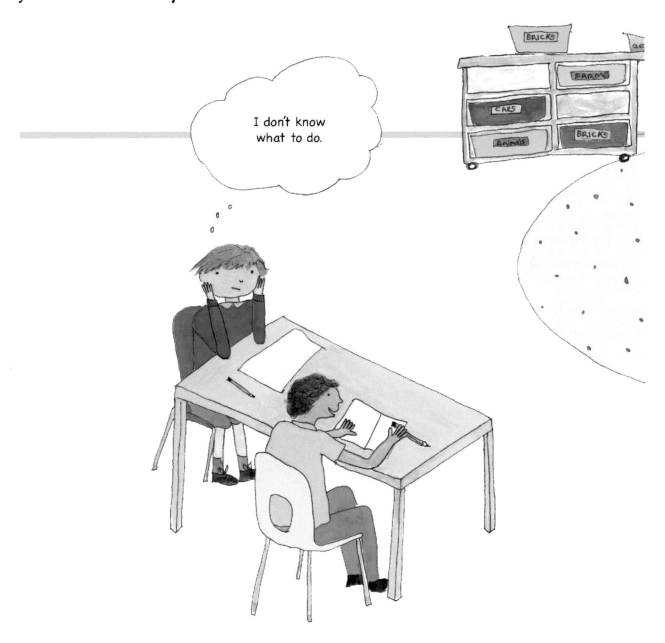

"It's time to write a story," he hears the others shout.

He's got some great ideas but he just can't get them out.

He looks down at his paper.
It stays as white as snow.

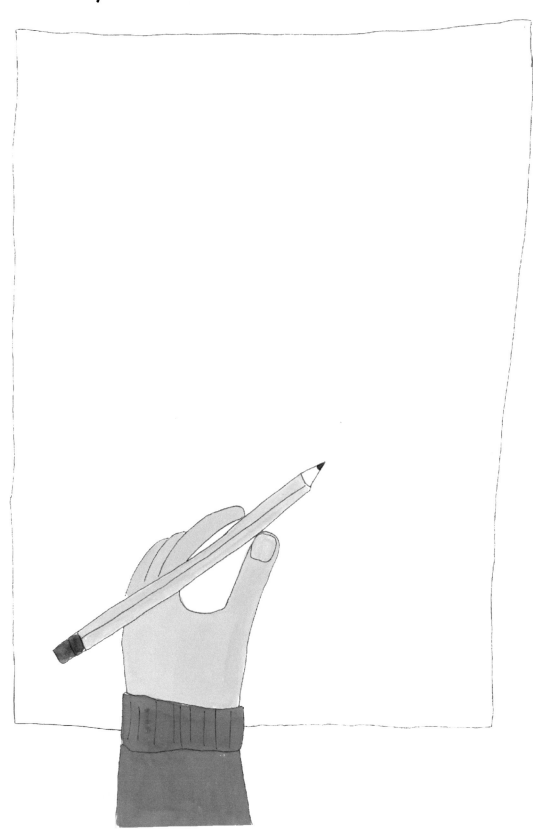

Letters and words are
difficult, but pictures
start to show.

He starts at the beginning, with a
brave and shining knight.

~~Cassl Man~~

~~Tin Man~~

~~Man~~

He can't think of the word
for knight ….

But he can draw one,
just right.

Next he draws a dragon,
sitting on the castle walls.

He's lost inside his story,
until his teacher calls.

"What are you doing Harry?
It's not the time to draw."

Harry feels embarrassed.
He looks down at the floor.

"My story got a dragon."
Harry tells Miss Heart.

"That one got some fire in him."
And he pointed to his art.

Miss Heart looked at his drawings

… and she saw the story flow.

She thought ....

"Those pictures help Harry.

I'm so glad that I know."

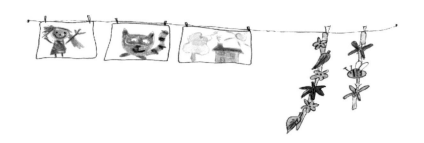

"Your dragon's breathing fire to
light the candles on a cake!
What a wonderful idea Harry.
I'm sorry for my mistake."

So Miss Heart changed her classroom.
There's pictures, paints and glue.
Now Harry smiles at story time
and he knows just what to do.